Great is the power of might and mind,
but only love can make us kind.
All we are or hope to be
is empty pride and vanity.
If love is not a part of all
the greatest man is very small.

Presented to

_____

from

_____

THE
Just Because
SERIES

Moments of Love

HELEN STEINER RICE

Fleming H. Revell
A Division of Baker Book House Co
Grand Rapids, Michigan 49516

© 2002 by Virginia Ruehlmann
and The Helen Steiner Rice Foundation

Published by Fleming H. Revell
a division of Baker Book House Company
P.O. Box 6287, Grand Rapids, MI 49516-6287

Poems taken from *Gifts of Love* by Helen Steiner Rice and Virginia Ruehlmann, published
in 1992, 2000. Biographical information drawn from *Helen Steiner Rice:
Ambassador of Sunshine* by Ronald Pollitt and Virginia Wiltse, published in 1994.

Printed in the United States of America

Library of Congress Cataloging-in-Publication Data is on file at the Library of Congress,
Washington, D.C.

ISBN 0-8007-1800-3

Cover photo ©Stuart Dee/getty images

Cover and interior design by Robin Black

For current information about all releases from Baker Book House, visit our web site:
http://www.bakerbooks.com

Love, Moment by Moment

The
Power of Love

Helen Steiner Rice was married just briefly, never had children, lived alone most of her life, and died as one of the last members of her family. Could this strong, single woman know much about love? She certainly did, according to the poems, books, letters, papers, and photos she left behind—and beyond that, as evidenced in the people she loved and those who loved her.

Tiny Helen, who stood a little over five feet tall, embodied a huge capacity for care and kindness, compassion and devotion. She was a powerhouse of love, defying all the stereotypes and showing how love changes everything—first the way you view the world, and in that process the way the world views you.

Love is a gift to treasure forever
  Given by God without price tag or measure.
  Love is a gift we all can possess,
  Love is a key to a soul's happiness!

The priceless gift of life is love,
  for with the help of God above,
Love can change the human race
  and make this world a better place.
For love dissolves all hate and fear
  and makes our vision bright and clear
So we can see and rise above
  our pettiness on wings of love.

This brings you a million good wishes and more
For the things you cannot buy in a store—
A joy-filled heart and a happy smile,
Faith to sustain you in times of trial,
Contentment, inner peace, and love—
All priceless gifts from God above!

With our hands we give gifts
    that money can buy—
Diamonds that sparkle
    like stars in the sky,
Trinkets that glitter
    like the sun as it rises,
Beautiful baubles
    that come as surprises—
But only our hearts
    can feel real love
And share the gift
    of our Father above.

What is love? No words can define it—
It's something so great only God could design it.
Wonder of wonders, beyond our conception,
And only in God can love find true perfection.
For love means much more than small words can express,
For what we call love is so very much less
Than the beauty and depth and the true richness of
God's gift to mankind—His compassionate love.
For love has become a word that's misused,
Perverted, distorted, and often abused
To speak of light romance or some affinity for
A passing attraction that is seldom much more
Than a mere interlude or inflamed fascination,
A romantic fling of no lasting duration.

But love is enduring and patient and kind,
It judges all things with the heart, not the mind.
And love can transform the most commonplace
Into beauty and splendor and sweetness and grace,
For love is unselfish—giving more than it takes—
And no matter what happens, love never forsakes.
It's faithful and trusting and always believing,
Guileless and honest and never deceiving.
Yes, love is beyond what we can define,
For love is immortal and God's gift is divine.

Every day is a reason for giving,
And giving is the key to living.
So let us give ourselves away,
Not just today but every day,
And remember, a kind and thoughtful deed
Or a hand outstretched in a time of need
Is the rarest of gifts, for it is a part
Not of the purse but a loving heart.
And those who give of themselves will find
True joy of heart and peace of mind.

Romance and
Commitments

From youth, even up to her death when frail and confined to her bed, Helen flirted with life and wrote from her soul about passions that endure circumstance and time. A self-confessed romantic, she admitted she was most prolific when asked at her day job of crafting greeting cards to write love poems. She penned thousands, sometimes with school-girl idealism and other times with a heavy dose of reality and candor. One of the latter, for example, for an unidentified beau, shows her practical humor about even the most romantic of relationships:

> Sometimes I like you,
> Sometimes I don't,
> Sometimes I could,
> Sometimes I won't,
>
> 'Cause if you're for me, and I'm for you,
> In spite of all that we say or do,
> We'll marry and live to say, "What luck!"
> Or regret it forever because we got stuck.

But in love Helen never found herself stuck. Romance and commitments endure, she believed. Though she shared less than four years with her husband amid the Great Depression, she held fast to their memory. She reread his letters over the years and confessed to friends even four decades later, "I go on honoring him—respecting him and loving him."

There are things we cannot measure,
   like the depths of waves and sea
And the heights of stars in heaven
   and the joy you bring to me.
Like eternity's long endlessness
   and the sunset's golden hue,
There is no way to measure
   the love I have for you.

Dear God,

Please help me in my feeble way
To somehow do something each day
To show the one I love the best
My faith in him will stand each test.
And let me show in some small way
The love I have for him each day
And prove beyond all doubt and fear
That his love for me I hold most dear.
And so I ask of God above—
Just make me worthy of his love.

Happy little memories

go flitting through my mind,
And in all my thoughts and memories
I always seem to find
The picture of your face, dear,
the memory of your touch
And all the other little things
I've come to love so much.
You cannot go beyond my thoughts
or leave my love behind,
Because I keep you in my heart
and forever in my mind.
And though I may not tell you,
I think you know it's true
That I find daily happiness
in the very thought of you.

There's a heap of satisfaction
to sit here thinking of you
And to tell you once again, dear,
how very much I love you.
There is comfort just in longing
for a smile from your dear face
And joy in just remembering
each sweet and fond embrace.
There is happiness in knowing
that my heart will always be
A place where I can hold you
and keep you near to me.

You put *love* in loveliness
    and the *sweet* in sweetness, too.
  I think they took life's dearest things
    and wrapped them up in you.
  And when I send good wishes,
    they're filled with love so true,
  And I hope the year will bring you
    the joy that is your due.
  For when I think of you, dear,
    I can't forget the thought
  Of how much real, true happiness
    just knowing you has brought.

In my eyes there lies no vision
    but the sight of your dear face,
In my heart there is no feeling
    but the warmth of your embrace
In my mind there are no thoughts
    but thoughts of you, my dear,
In my soul, no other longing
    but just to have you near.
All my dreams are built around you,
    and I've come to know it's true—
In my life there is no living
    that is not a part of you.

Imagine a bee without a beehive,
A dog without his bark,
A skate without its rollers,
A bench without a park,
A boat without an ocean,
A dove without its coo,
And you can imagine
The way I feel without you.

Like a puppy needs its biscuits,
Like a kitten needs its cream,
Like a mouse needs Roquefort,
Like a parrot needs its scream,
Like a horse needs its nose-bag,
Like a cow needs her chew,
Like a monkey needs a coconut,
That's how I need you!

I think of you so many times
and wish with all my heart
That I could reach across the miles
that keep us far apart
And somehow just communicate
the things I'd like to say
If I were standing close to you
instead of far away.

Love is a many-splendored thing,
the greatest joy that life can bring,
And let no one try to disparage
the sacred bond of holy marriage,
For love is not love until God above
sanctifies the union of two people in love.

What is marriage?

It is sharing and caring,
giving and forgiving,
loving and being loved,
walking hand in hand,
talking heart to heart,
seeing through each other's eyes,
laughing together,
weeping together,
praying together,
and always trusting and believing
and thanking God for each other.
For love that is shared is a beautiful thing,
It enriches the soul and makes the heart sing.

Love is much more than a tender caress
    and more than bright hours of happiness,
For a lasting love is made up of sharing
    both hours that are joyous and also despairing.
It's made up of patience and deep understanding
    and never of stubborn or selfish demanding.
It's made up of climbing the steep hills together
    and facing with courage life's stormiest weather.
Nothing on earth or in heaven can part
    a love that has grown to be part of the heart,
And just like the sun and the stars and the sea,
    this love will go on through eternity,
For true love lives on when earthly things die,
    for it's part of the spirit that soars to the sky.

Family Love

Neither time, nor distance—nor even blood relation—kept Helen from declaring her love for those she called "family."

She wrote poems of adoration for her beloved Grandmother Beieri, who taught her Scriptures and told the stories Helen remembered all through life. Her anthem of love upon her mother's passing in 1945 became a best-selling card of sympathy. Her devotion to fellow employees caught in company downsizings in the '50s and '60s elicited more verses of comfort and care.

"Happiness is only found in bringing it to others," she wrote, "and thinking of the folks next door as sisters and as brothers."

Our Father, who art in heaven,
 hear this little prayer
And reach across the miles today
 that stretch from here to there,
So I may feel much closer
 to those I'm fondest of,
And they may know I think of them
 with thankfulness and love.
And help all people everywhere
 who must often dwell apart
To know that they're together
 in the haven of the heart.

The dearest gifts that heaven holds,
    the very finest, too,
Were made into one pattern
    that was perfect, sweet, and true.
The angels smiled, well pleased, and said,
    "Compared to all the others,
This pattern is so wonderful
    let's use it just for mothers!"
And through the years, a mother
    has been all that's sweet and good,
For there's a bit of God and love
    in all true motherhood.

A mother's love is something
that no one can explain—
It is made of deep devotion
and of sacrifice and pain.
It is endless and unselfish
and enduring, come what may,
For nothing can destroy it
or take the love away.
It is patient and forgiving
when all others are forsaking.
And it never fails or falters
even though the heart is breaking.

It believes beyond believing
  when the world around condemns,
And it glows with all the beauty
  of the rarest, brightest gems,
It is far beyond defining,
  it defies all explanation,
And it still remains a secret
  like the mysteries of creation—
A many-splendored miracle
  we cannot understand
And another wondrous evidence
  of God's tender, guiding hand.

Our Father in heaven,
   whose love is divine,
Thanks for the love
   of a mother like mine.
In Thy great mercy
   look down from above
And grant this dear mother
   the gift of Your love,
And all through the year,
   whatever betide her,
Assure her each day
   that You are beside her.
And Father in heaven,
   show me the way
To lighten her tasks
   and brighten her day.
And bless her dear heart
   with the insight to see
That her love means more
   than the world to me.

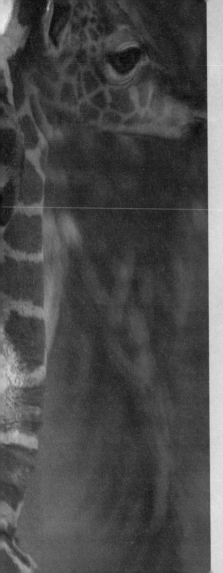

On Mother's Day my thoughts go back
  to all the years that have gone before,
And all of my love and good wishes
  go straight to that open door.
For always the door to your heart and home
  stood open with welcoming cheer,
And memories of you, Grandmother,
  grow dearer with each year.

Loving cost Helen Steiner Rice. Repeatedly in life she lost those she loved most: Upon high school graduation, her father. Upon marriage, her husband. Upon a skyrocketing career, her mother; at a time of fading health, her oldest and dearest friends.

But she discovered one love that gave more than it ever exacted. "The only thing that can lift me above my earthly bondage is to be alone with God," she explained in a letter to a friend. He not only mends hearts but the reparation enlarges the heart, making it better able to carry a deeper love in a larger way.

For the remainder of her life, Helen focused on articulating the nature of this most pure, divine, and selfless of loves. She also savored the word picture penned by Edwin Markham, an author who lost his fortune through some unfortunate investments. Markham wrestled with resentment toward those he felt had wronged him. His anger boiled into an ugly bitterness—so bitter, so ugly that it consumed his thoughts and energy. Soon, he realized, the anger was hurting him more than any financial loss. Toying with this thought and a pencil at the same time, Markham began to draw two interlocking circles. The doodle inspired perhaps his most remembered verse:

> He drew a circle that shut me out,
> Heretic, rebel, a thing to flout;
> But love and I had the wit to win:
> We drew a circle that took him in.

The love of God
is too great to conceive.
Don't try to explain it—
just trust and believe!

God, be my resting place and my protection
in hours of trouble, defeat, and dejection.
May I never give way to self-pity and sorrow,
may I always be sure of a better tomorrow.
May I stand undaunted, come what may,
secure in the knowledge I have only to pray
And ask my Creator and Father above
to keep me serene in His grace and His love.

It can't be bought, it can't be sold,
It can't be measured in silver and gold.
It's a special wish that God above
Will fill your heart with peace and love—
The love of God, which is divine,
That is beyond what words can define
So you may know the comfort of
God's all-fulfilling grace and love.

God is love,
and He made the human heart
capable of this great miracle of love
so that we might glimpse heaven
and experience that divine touch.

I come not to ask, to plead, or implore You,
   I just come to tell You how much I adore You.
For to kneel in Your presence makes me feel blessed,
   for I know that You know all my needs best,
And it fills me with joy just to linger with You,
   as my soul You replenish and my heart You renew.
For prayer is much more than just asking for things—
   it's the peace and contentment that quietness brings.
So thank You again for Your mercy and love
   and for making me heir to Your kingdom above.

Lord, show me the way I can somehow repay
    the blessings You've given to me.
  Lord, teach me to do what You most want me to
    and to be what You want me to be.
  I'm unworthy, I know, but I do love You so,
    I beg You to answer my plea.
  I've not much to give, but as long as I live
    may I give it completely to Thee.

Dear God, You are a part of me,
You're all I hear and all I see.
You're what I say and what I do
For all my life belongs to You.
You walk with me and You talk with me,
For I am Yours eternally.
And when I stumble, slip, and fall
Because I'm weak and lost and small,
You help me up and take my hand
And lead me toward the Promised Land.
I cannot dwell apart from You,
You would not ask or want me to,
For You have room within Your heart
To make each child of Yours a part
Of You and all Your love and care,
For God, You are love and
    love should be everywhere!

Whatever the celebration, whatever the day, whatever the event or occasion, Helen Steiner Rice possessed the ability to express the appropriate feeling for that particular moment. A happening became happier, a sentiment more sentimental, a memory more memorable because of her deep sensitivity and ability to put into understandable language the emotion being experienced. Her positive attitude, concern for others, and love of God are identifiable threads woven into her life, work, and even her death.

Just before her passing, she established the Helen Steiner Rice Foundation. Because of limited resources, the Foundation presently limits grants to qualified charitable programs in Lorain, Ohio, where she lived and worked most of her life. It's the Foundation's hope that in the future resources will be of sufficient size that broader geographical areas may be considered in the awarding of grants.

Because of her foresight, caring, and deep conviction of sharing, Helen Steiner Rice continues to touch a countless number of lives through Foundation grants and through her inspirational poetry.

Thank you for your help to keep Helen's dream alive and growing.

ANDREA E. CORNETT, ADMINISTRATOR
THE HELEN STEINER RICE FOUNDATION